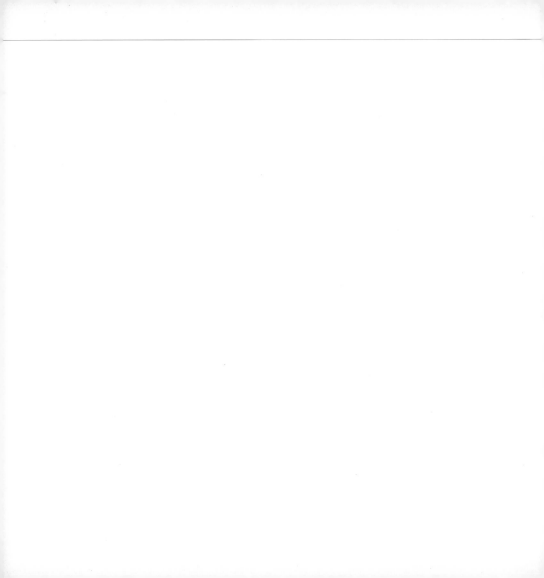

MOTHER KNOWS BEST

Created by
Dean Buckhorn and Scott Gardiner

Andrews McMeel
Publishing

Kansas City

04 05 06 07 08 WKT 10 9 8 7 6 5 4 3 2 1

ISBN: 0-7407-4163-2

Library of Congress Control Number: 2003111241

WELCOME TO

the mountain of laundry, dusting, and dishes known as

MOM'S LIFE

MAYBE I'LL GROW

four extra arms so I'll actually have enough time to plant

A GARDEN!

IT'S GOOD TO

have three nannies, a maid, and an in-home psychiatrist if you plan to

BE A MOTHER!

MOTHERHOOD

makes you tired, cranky, and old. Plastic surgery

KEEPS YOU YOUNG

EVERY DAY IS

a never-ending list of chores that earns you "oh boy!" a box of candy on

MOTHER'S DAY

MOM BAKED

so many macaroni and cheese dinners, she's about to toss her

COOKIES

LET MOMMY

know if anyone's dead or bleeding, otherwise you kids

HANDLE IT

HAPPINESS IS

realizing that eventually the kids will go off to college and you'll have

A CLEAN HOUSE

MY KIDS ARE
louder and messier than a roomful of Hell's
ANGELS

IT'S SO FUN

watching your husband's feeble attempts

TO BE A MOM

HAPPINESS IS
all the stuff you can't do because you're too busy
BEING A MOM

DARLING, I
think hell would freeze over if I actually
BAKED A PIE

NO DUST BUNNIES

will be vacuumed up anytime soon

IN MY HOUSE

MOMS LOVE

to fantasize about a long, restful holiday without

THEIR KIDS

YES, DINNER

is burned to a crisp because Mommy

IS COOKED

DO I HAVE TIME TO
run screaming out of the house before I have to
CLEAN THE BATHROOM?

MOTHER
does all the work, but Father still thinks he
KNOWS BEST

MOTHERHOOD

is a twenty-four-hour job, and getting a good night's sleep

IS JUST A DREAM

MY OVEN

hasn't been used in months so no wonder it

IS SPOTLESS

HOUSEWORK IS

such a low-paying job that it makes panhandling look

VERY REWARDING

NO, HONEY,

you just sit on your lazy butt like always and

I'LL DO IT!

HUSBANDS

are those beer-guzzling couch potatoes who think they

ARE A DREAM

HOUSEWORK IS A
huge pain in the butt that only a man would call a
LABOR OF LOVE!

HONEY, HOW WAS

that eight-hour snooze-fest in a cushy office that you call

WORK TODAY?

OH BOY, I GET TO

slave over a hot oven because no one else knows how to

COOK DINNER!

IT'S FUN TO BE

home all day but this housework stuff can be

A REAL MOTHER

YES, IT'S A
tough job pretending that picking up dirty socks is a
WONDERFUL LIFE

HAPPINESS IS

dreaming about bulldozing the entire house instead of

TIDYING UP!

A CLEAN HOUSE IS
pretty much out of the question. I'll settle for
A HAPPY HOUSE!

THERE'S NO PLACE

except maybe boot camp that can exhaust a mother

LIKE HOME!

SURE KIDS, I'LL

register you for military school and then I'll

DRIVE YOU THERE!

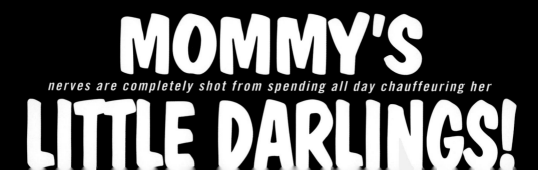

MOMMY'S

nerves are completely shot from spending all day chauffeuring her

LITTLE DARLINGS!

WHICH WAY TO

the sofa, the den, please anywhere but

THE KITCHEN?

I LOVE THE
cute bag boys at the
GROCERY STORE!

OH GOLLY, IT'S
the eight hours of smelling dirty socks otherwise known as
LAUNDRY DAY!

CAN I GET YOU

to pick up your dirty socks before I smother you with

A PILLOW?